DUMP THAT CHUMP

A Ten-Step Plan to Ending Bad Relationships and Attracting the Fabulous Partner You Deserve

Other Books by Esther Kane:

What Your Mama Can't or Won't Teach You: Grown Women's Stories of Their Teen Years

Available at: www.guidebooktowomanhood.com

DUMP THAT CHUMP

A Ten-Step Plan to Ending Bad Relationships and Attracting the Fabulous Partner You Deserve

By Esther Kane, MSW, Registered Clinical Counsellor
www.estherkane.com
www.dumpthatchump.com

Canadian Cataloguing in Publication Data

Kane, Esther, 1971-
Dump that chump : a ten-step plan for ending bad relationships and attracting the fabulous partner you deserve / Esther Kane.

ISBN 0-9780706-1-5

1. Mate selection. 2. Abused women--Psychology. I. Title.

HQ801.K33 2006   646.7'7082   C2006-903416-8

If you would like to publish sections of this book, please contact the publisher for permission.

Published by:

Esther Kane, MSW, RCC
250.338.1800
www.estherkane.com
esther@estherkane.com

Design and cover art by nrichmedia (www.nrichmedia.com).

Dedication

To my darling husband, Nathaniel, who is most definitely, NOT a "chump."

You are the greatest gift in my life. You've proven to me that healthy, loving,

and fulfilling relationships are worth working for! Thanks for giving me the

love and roots I needed to soar and become the woman I was meant to be.

Your love heals and nurtures me every step along the way.

TABLE OF CONTENTS

INTRODUCTION

The title of this book was taken from one of my favourite blues songs from "Saffire: The Uppity Blues Women." The singer bellows out, "Dump that chump. You'd better lose that loser. You'd better listen to me."

I think these women are onto something when it comes to intimate relationships and the bad choices we often make. I can't tell you how many women have come to see me for counselling because they are miserable in the relationship they're currently in, or are recovering from one they've just extricated themselves from. All of these women, by the way, happen to be highly intelligent, funny, attractive, and successful in nearly every other area in their lives. So why do they keep picking the wrong mate? How is it that we women can be so intelligent and successful in our lives and yet when it comes to relationships, we pick the losers?

Believe me, I understand all too well as I was one of those women for a long time myself. It took a very painful and scary experience with an abusive man before I finally woke up to the fact that I was choosing the wrong guys. I'm definitely not recommending this style of learning as it is extremely traumatic and has long-lasting aftereffects.

However, I decided to use this tragic life experience as an opportunity to learn how and why I had created this pattern of dating people who weren't good for me. I spent the next five years deliberately single so that I could focus all of my energy on healing myself, figuring out why I had such a tough time with relation-ships, and gaining the skills and tools I needed in order to pick someone someday who was perfect for me.

After following the steps I'm about to share with you, I met the love of my life. That was almost eight years ago and we are still totally in love and very happy together. You see; I had worked so hard on becoming the kind of woman who would attract such a person, along with visualizing who that person would be, that it actually wasn't a huge surprise when he came into my life.

I liken the experience to being prepared for an exam: You study like mad until you're confident when the day finally arrives and you are prepared for it. When you breeze through and get a great mark, you feel good, but you also realize that you earned it because you worked so hard for it.

Through my own life experience, as well as from counselling a multitude of women from all ages and backgrounds, I have come to some conclusions about why we choose the partners we do and how we can change those patterns for the better if they are no longer working for us. Experience tells me that these themes are true for the majority of women out there, regardless of one's sexual orientation. Whether you are straight, gay, or bi-sexual, I am confident that you will find this book of immense help in finding your ideal partner.

The book is divided into two main parts. The first part focuses on how we got to where we are today with regards to relationships and choosing partners. In this section, I aim to shed some light onto why we often pick the wrong mates. In short, I have found that most women pick the wrong mate(s) because of our false beliefs about who we are and what we deserve in life. These come from our growing-up years. The focus will be on the main forces that shape us in those early years: our family-of-origin, ethnicity and culture, and the influence of the larger society in which we live.

I will also share with you *what we end up doing* with what we've learned from our family-of-origin, along with the societal influences, and how we entrap ourselves way into adulthood, even when we've supposedly 'grown up' and would rather not be so influenced by our upbringing.

In the second part, the focus will be on giving you, the reader, necessary tools to get "unstuck" so that you can move forward in the realm of intimate relationships and find yourself one day in the wonderful and fulfilling relationship you want and deserve. Throughout the book, I will give you real-life examples from my own, and from my clients' lives, which will inspire you and give you confidence in your quest for fulfilling relationships. My clients are my greatest teachers, and it is through witnessing their struggles and growth that I am able to pass on this wisdom.

I want to thank the incredible women that I have worked with for sharing their courageous journeys with me and for being able to offer the lessons learned in order to help other women. I believe so much in the power of sharing stories, for in doing so, we guide and inspire one another in becoming all we dream of being. Thank you to all women who come across my path as I heal, grow, and become the woman that the Creator intended me to be. It is an honour to know you, share with you, and to walk alongside you. You are all my angels and teachers. Thank you also to my grandmother, mother, and sister – you have given me the wings I needed to fly. I am so grateful to have you in my life.

Esther

PART 1:
HOW WE GOT HERE AND WHAT KEEPS US STUCK

Family-of-Origin

I chose to be trained as a family systems therapist because I believe that what we learn from our families growing up are the most powerful indicators of how we will turn out as adults. How does this relate to how we choose our mates? Let me give you some examples.

"Sue" came to see me because she had just left her alcoholic and abusive spouse and was traumatized by years of living with the chaos created by alcoholism and abuse. She described herself as "depressed." She felt lost and was trying to sort out her life and start over again. When we explored family-of-origin experiences, it turned out that her father was an alcoholic and had been abusive to her mother. Throughout the course of therapy, Sue came to understand that her role model for men growing up had been her father. While he was anything but perfect, his *type* of "man" was what she knew and felt comfortable with.

When she met the man who would later become her husband, she felt "at home" with him. While his drinking and abusive behaviour eventually became intolerable, she was initially attracted to what she "knew best" on a subconscious level.

Don't get me wrong – I'm not implying that Sue wasn't an intelligent woman because she picked the wrong mate. This choosing process has *nothing to do with intellect.* If we haven't done a lot of working through early family-of-origin experiences and come to realize how they have shaped our current beliefs and behaviours, we're bound to go for what is most familiar.

The sad fact is that many of us are familiar with the types of people and behaviours that make us the most miserable and which leave us feeling unfulfilled. But we keep on choosing them out of habit. It's what we *learn to expect in life* that gets us into trouble. Sue had the experience of having an alcoholic father who treated her and her mother badly. He was a role model for how men behaved when she was growing up, so she tended to believe that *all men* behaved like her father. I have come up with a catchy phrase that helps a lot of my clients to move forward:

WHAT YOU EXPECT IS WHAT YOU GET.

Sue got exactly what she expected when she met – and later married – her husband. Did it make her happy and fulfill her needs for an intimate relationship? NO. Was it familiar to her and was it what she expected? YES. There is a very big difference between the two.

See, the thing is we don't like to live in the world of the 'unfamiliar.' Many of us like to feel SAFE. We like our lives and the people in them to be PREDICTABLE. When we don't know what to expect, we get the "jitters" and are no longer in our comfort zone. This anxiety is uncomfortable and in order to get rid of it, we go back to where we feel safe and comfortable. When Sue met her husband, he was familiar to her. She was comfortable because she knew what she could expect from him and from the relationship.

I often tell clients that we're not afraid of the things we think we are. We're afraid of what we DON'T KNOW and what is unfamiliar to us. Up until my late 20s, I kept picking guys who were emotionally unavailable and who often had addictions to alcohol, drugs, and/or food. I was constantly miserable and knew in my heart that these were not potential life-partners; but was clueless as to why I kept picking the same kind of guy and how to stop from doing so in future relationships.

It wasn't until I did some intensive therapy and looked at my family-of-origin, that I found the answers I was looking for. Most of the men in my life were emotionally unavailable, due to various addictions. Unfortunately, none of them ever received treatment for their addictions. The women in my life accepted their behaviour as normal so I, in turn, did the same.

It quickly became clear to me that I kept picking the same type of man over and over again. I knew addiction. I knew abandonment. I knew men who didn't respect or appreciate women and treated them badly. Guys like that (even though they made me miserable), were familiar and within my comfort zone. I knew what to expect from them and I got it every time.

WHAT I EXPECTED WAS EXACTLY WHAT I GOT.

Ethnicity/Culture and the Larger Society in Which We Live

While our family-of-origin has a huge impact on how we choose future partners, so do our ethnicity, culture, and the larger society in which we live. For example, I had an Indo-Canadian client once who came to see me after her husband had been removed from the family home by the police because of his violent behaviour towards his wife and two children.

While it was appallingly clear to outsiders that her husband was dangerous and a serious threat to her and the children, she still felt badly about leaving him because as a woman in a Muslim community, she would be shunned for doing so. As well, she and the children would be isolated from their religious and cultural group as a result. When she did decide to leave and protect herself and her children, that's exactly what happened. Her entire community shunned her and the children because they judged her as being "wrong" for leaving her husband, even when they knew what he had done. She was taught by her religious and cultural upbringing that divorce was wrong and that men were allowed to abuse their wives.

This woman had the courage to face being publicly ostracized and cut off from her entire community in order to save her life and protect her children from a very dangerous man who could have one day taken their lives. It took months of therapy to support her through this transition and to give her the message that she had a right to do what she did and deserved to be treated well.

Also, within the larger North American culture, women are bombarded by unwritten rules of conduct and faulty beliefs about ourselves that really get in the way of feeling that we have the right to healthy, loving, and fulfilling relationships. Some that come readily to mind that I hear almost daily from clients are:

- We have to be "nice" at all costs, even if someone treats us badly

- Men and women really are "different species" and we can't expect to have wonderful relationships between the two

- If I say what I want and need from another person, I'm being 'selfish'

- If you want to have children, you can't always be picky about the mate you choose – the clock is ticking!

- We're supposed to do the all the work in relationships and put up with whatever that person brings to it

- Relationships are difficult and you have to suffer if you want to be loved

- I can't expect a great relationship, so I'll take what I can get

I could go on, but I'm sure you get the point and can come up with some of your own as well. Compound that with pathetic "love" songs with lyrics that suggest that "love hurts" and that you're supposed to lose yourself and morph into a single co-dependent blob when two people become a couple, things look grim! This is nothing new, either. In the 1930's, Billie Holiday was singing, "My man he beats me. He treats me awful mean... But I love him…" When I hear that, I scream to the stereo, "Leave him Billie! You deserve better! Love doesn't have to hurt!"

My view is that, basically, girls and women are given very bad role models for relationships from the people they are in close contact with and the larger community outside. This is terribly sad because what ends up happening when we believe what we see and are told about relationships is that we unconsciously create more of the same. If we see abuse and are taught that it's acceptable, we end up in abusive relationships later on. If one of our parents is an alcoholic when we are growing up, we have a *98% chance* of choosing an alcoholic or chemically dependent mate when we are adults.

This creates a vicious cycle that is bound to repeat itself unless we consciously intervene and change things in a radical way. The good news is that we *can* and that countless women, regardless of what they were taught growing up, have chosen to have healthy, loving, and fulfilling relationships in their adult lives and have wonderful mates. I have done this and so can you! It just takes some education, self-work, a sense of humour, and time...

What We Say to Ourselves

After examining our family-of-origin, as well as the larger culture and the ethnicity we come from, it becomes obvious that we have received many messages about relationships and how they should be done. As children, we're like 'little sponges' for other people's beliefs, values, and worldviews and we 'soak up' this information in our little brains and go forth into the world and act according to what we see as "reality."

Also, as children, we're not usually cognizant of the fact that this so-called "reality" isn't ours; that it's made up of other people's belief systems and life experiences. It is only when we become adults that we start questioning this stuff and when we're teens, we often say, "Stick your 'reality' where the sun don't shine! I'm doing it my way!" As wonderful as this may feel, we often act this way as teens as a form of rebellion, and haven't consciously *chosen* to do things differently from our elders.

However, as adults, we have the amazing opportunity to re-examine what we've been taught, take what we like, discard what we don't, and replace it with something that works better for us. That's where this book comes in. Through reading it, and doing the exercises contained within its pages, I hope that you will be gently guided through this process in the area of intimate relationships and, hopefully, you'll be pleased with the results.

In this last section before you start doing the work, I want to talk to you about the messages *we give to ourselves* that keep us stuck in unfulfilling relationships. I believe that this is the point in therapy where 'the rubber hits the road' and that this is the most important area to work on changing because without changing what we tell ourselves about relationships, we're doomed to repeat history. And that, as we all now know, sure ain't no picnic! If it were working for you so far, you wouldn't be reading this book, would you?

Without giving you a bunch of useless "psychobabble," I'll simply say that *what we tell ourselves, we get.* You see, the brain isn't as smart as we think it is. What I mean by that is **your mind believes what you tell it.**

For example, if you tell yourself that there are no great potential partners out there, then what do you think you're going to get? A great partner? I think not!

When you tell yourself this, your brain basically says, "Okay then. We won't bother looking for someone good. We'll just take whatever comes our way." Then you end up 'settling' for someone who isn't great for you and you've proved to yourself that you were right! Not much of a prize for being right, is it?

Throughout this book, I am inviting you to 'try on' some different thinking about relationships in order to expand the realm of what is possible for yourself *in* relationships. I realize that this can be scary and it might even induce thoughts of, "Who the hell does she think she is, telling me this?" but that's a good sign.

As a therapist, my job is to gently "nudge" people to unexplored places that may alleviate suffering and give them a lot more pleasure in life. At first, people resist like crazy (sometimes, even discontinuing our work together), but if they are able to stay with it and move past their discomfort, the most amazing things happen.

I have seen countless women face their fear, do the work, and permanently rid themselves of unsatisfying relationships. I get to enjoy witnessing their bliss in their new, loving, and very fulfilling relationships that emerge as a result of their hard work. Not one of these women has ever told me that it wasn't worth doing the work for!

So in writing this book, I aim to "nudge" you a bit in order to help you find the joy and satisfaction you want in your intimate relationships. The only thing I ask from you in order to do this is to try and keep an open mind and remember that **_change is scary_** for all of us. It's hard to examine your relationship patterns under a microscope and try new things in order to do it differently. But when the going gets tough, I urge you to remind yourself of the alternative: **staying stuck in miserable relationships for the rest of your years**. Does *that* thought motivate you to at least *try*?

Why do I give you such an upsetting image to ponder? Because research shows that people often aren't motivated to make significant life changes until they're scared into it. A good example is the guy whose diet consisted of burgers and fries and other junk food, who all-of-a-sudden nearly dies because of clogged arteries. A stint of triple-bypass surgery can be great motivation to change one's eating habits! Two weeks after surgery, this same man is seen consuming vast amounts of salad, fruit, and whole grains. Why? He was motivated to change by thinking about the alternative!

Ditto with relationships. If you've bought this book, I'm assuming that your experience in relationships up until this point hasn't been the most enjoyable and you're willing to try something new in order to change all that. Now is the perfect time to get unstuck!

PART 2:
HOW TO GET UNSTUCK

Let's Get to It!

In this section, I want you to roll up your sleeves and do some hard but extremely rewarding work. Are you ready to let go of being with the wrong partner and suffering in relationships? Yes? Then let's get to work!

I suggest that you do the exercises in this section right in this book. To make this easy for you, I have left plenty of space for your answers underneath each question. To make things even easier, I will use a fictitious client – I'll call her "Jean" – as an example to illustrate answers to all of the questions. These answers will probably be a lot shorter than yours as I just want to give you an idea of what is being asked in each question.

One last reminder, before you get going:

WHAT YOU EXPECT IS WHAT YOU GET.

Let's start changing our expectations in order to get what we want and need in relationships...

Step One: Make a Commitment to Yourself

In the first step, I want to present a somewhat radical idea: **Committing to yourself the way you would like a partner to commit to you someday.** This is not my idea. I first found it in a wonderful book written by SARK called *Transformation Soup* (pg.37, Simon & Schuster, 2000). I highly recommend any of SARK's books as they are fun, creative, and full of great ideas. Her books can be found online at www.planetsark.com.

In *Transformation Soup*, SARK talks about "marrying yourself." I read this when I was 21 and leaving a very abusive relationship, and just before I left for good, I had a "marrying myself" ceremony with some close girlfriends. I believe that it was this ceremony, along with the incredible love and support I received from my friends, that gave me the strength to finally leave.

Although it may sound trite, I sincerely believe that we can only truly love another person (and be fully loved by them) once we love ourselves. How can we attract a fabulous partner if we don't believe that we, too, are fabulous and worth spending the rest of our lives with?

To get you started, I want you to get into the mood of the whole idea of loving/marrying yourself by answering the following questions in great detail... These come from a workshop that a dear friend of mine, Michelle Crowley, MA, and I did in Vancouver for women a number of years ago.

"How Do I Love Me?" Questions

1. If I were to marry myself, what kind of commitment ceremony would I want?

2. Who would I invite?

3. What would my vows be?

4. Where would my ceremony take place?

5. Describe the food, music, and festivities in detail.

6. What would I wear?

7. Where would I take myself for a honeymoon?

"How Do I Love Me?" Exercises

1. **Buy or make a Valentine's Day card for yourself for next Valentine's.** In it, write advice for yourself on how you can love yourself more. Fill it up! Make sure to mail it to yourself (no, I'm not kidding!) just before Valentine's and then read it to yourself when it arrives in the mail!

2. **On a piece of fancy stationary, write yourself a love letter** – the kind that you dream of receiving from a 'special someone' someday. I suggest doing this when you have the space and time to indulge your fantasies and let loose. Here are the instructions:

Sit back and close your eyes. Imagine your dream lover… imagine the new self-loving, confident you and your dream lover exploring your passions and dreams together. After a particularly memorable night of passion, you lover is so moved, that s/he is compelled to write you a love letter. Now open your eyes and "channel" the worlds that this letter contains onto a blank page. Please feel free to embellish with perfume, lipstick kisses, rose petals, or whatever seems most romantic to your senses...

Once you have finished writing, take a stamped envelope, put your love letter inside, seal it, and address it to yourself. This is for your eyes only when it comes to your door... hide it somewhere special in your boudoir... read it when the mood hits!

Step Two: Do Some Family-of-Origin Work

Ideally, this is best done with a qualified therapist, in person. You can work with the following questions I've listed to get you started and/or seek a therapist who specializes in family systems therapy.

In this step, I want you to be COMPLETELY HONEST with yourself in writing the answers to the questions posed. When it comes to family; this is no small task because we have all of the "shoulds" and "shouldn'ts" rolling around in our heads when we start to say things as we see them/experienced them. This is completely normal. But remember: **You don't have to show your answers to anyone else.**

I encourage you to practice mindfulness when doing this exercise. By that, I mean just NOTICING those thoughts as you write, but not becoming attached to them. Remember, this is your version of what happened in the family; no one else's and as such, it is totally unique and will not be like anyone else's.

There are no "rights" or "wrongs" when it comes to personal reactions to things that happened in the past. In the mindfulness tradition, I encourage you to practice unconditional love and acceptance for yourself as you unearth your experiences of family and relationships. You're not doing this to judge or persecute anyone; just to help you understand why you've done things a certain way and to help you make useful changes in the future in those areas that aren't working so well for you now.

The point of this work is not to blame family members or to lash out at them for what they did and didn't teach us. The point is to heal ourselves and continue where our family left off, in order to become happier and healthier people in our relationships.

I've given you lots of space to write your answers and I encourage you to use all of it (and more in another notebook if necessary). The more you write, the more you will gain understanding, which will enable you to radically shift the way you do relationships in the future.

Family-of-Origin Questions About Relationships

1. Who were my primary role models for adult relationships in my family?

2. What did I learn about intimate relationships from the men in my family?

3. What did I learn about intimate relationships from the women in my family?

4. Did my parents have a healthy, loving, and rewarding relationship? Why? Why not?

5. Did my grandparents have healthy, loving, and rewarding relationships? Why? Why not?

6. What did my grandparents teach my parents about relationships and how they should be?

7. What did my parents do with that knowledge?

8. What happened when I started dating? How did my family react? What did they say to guide me or influence me in relationships?

9. How have my choices of partners as an adult been influenced by what I learned from my family-of-origin?

10. What are the things I learned about relationships from my family that *haven't* helped me in my adult life?

11. What are the things I learned about relationships from my family that *have* helped me in my adult life?

Jean's Answers

1. Who were my primary role models for adult relationships in my family?

My mom and dad.

My paternal and maternal grandparents.

2. What did I learn about intimate relationships from the men in my family?

I learned that men were the "providers" for the family and their job was to be out working all the time to pay for the family's expenses. My dad just went along with everything my mom said and seemed to think she was in charge of running the family. He didn't have to do too much except earn money.

3. What did I learn about intimate relationships from the women in my family?

I learned that women were the ones in a relationship to be emotional and to get upset or excited about things that happened in the family. My mother's job was to stay home and raise the kids and take care of the house. She wasn't expected to work outside the home. As long as the children were looked after, the house was clean, and the meals were made, she was doing her job well.

4. Did my parents have a healthy, loving, and rewarding relationship? Why? Why not?

Definitely not. I guess it wasn't abusive or anything, but it wasn't close either. My dad didn't talk a lot to my mother and didn't seem to be in love with her. He just ignored her if she was upset and she seemed to be closer to her girlfriends than to her own husband. I also remember they slept in separate beds when I was a teenager, so I don't know if they even had sex for a lot of the marriage which tells me they probably weren't that happy together.

5. Did my grandparents have healthy, loving, and rewarding relationships? Why? Why not?

I don't think so. I know that my grandfather drank a lot and was verbally abusive to his wife when he was drunk. He died in his early 60's from liver failure and my grandmother didn't seem devastated. In fact, she seemed a lot happier and started going on trips and stuff. They had six children and in those days, the wife stayed home and raised the kids and the husband worked. I don't think they even thought about whether they were "in love" — it was more of a practical arrangement. I know they didn't have a lot of fun times together and things were really tense in the home when the kids were growing up.

6. What did my grandparents teach my parents about relationships and how they should be?

They taught my parents that a relationship (in this case, a marriage) was a practical arrangement where the man and the woman each have their roles and that by following these rules life would be fine.

7. What did my parents do with that knowledge?

They just followed that advice and the examples they were given and recreated a relationship very similar to the ones their parents had.

8. What happened when I started dating? How did my family react? What did they say to guide me or influence me in relationships?

My parents were really overprotective of me and wouldn't let me be alone with a guy until I went to university. They told me that most boys were "after one thing only" and that I should be careful and not give them what they want

until I'm married. They expected me to get married and have children and to
never get divorced.

9. How have my choices of partners as an adult been influenced by what I learned from my family-of-origin?

I listened to what they told me and followed their example, and ended up in a
miserable marriage for 12 years. I picked a man just like my dad and I
became just like my mother and I couldn't stand it. Even though he was what
I expected, I didn't really enjoy him as a person and I definitely wasn't in love
with him.

10. What are the things I learned about relationships from my family that *haven't* helped me in my adult life?

- *Relationships are just practical; that you don't need to be in love with*
  the person you marry

- *That you should stay together even if you're miserable together*

- *That men and women have defined and rigid roles and should stick to them even if they don't make them happy or fulfilled*

11. What are the things I learned about relationships from my family that *have* helped me in my adult life?

- *To not give up when things get hard*

- *That raising children is important and it's important to do a good job*

Step Three: Re-examine Your Beliefs and Value Systems

One of the most important factors in finding the right mate is to know yourself through and through. Only when we are totally clear on who we are, including the most vital aspects of ourselves – i.e., our beliefs and values – will we know exactly what we are looking for in a partner. In other words, the best "fit" for us will ultimately be somebody who has the same beliefs and values as we do.

To help you in this process of deeply examining your inner self, I have come up with some vital questions that will leave you with a clear sense of what you are all about and, therefore, what you are looking for in a mate.

Beliefs and Value Systems Questions About Relationships

1. What did I learn from my religion and/or culture(s) I grew up in about intimate relationships?

2. What was my expected role in relationships as a woman?

3. What was I taught by my religion and/or culture(s) to expect and not expect in relationships?

4. What was I taught by my religion and/or culture(s) about what would happen to me if I didn't abide by their rules/beliefs/values about relationships?

5. How have my choices of partners as an adult been influenced by what I learned from my religion and/or culture(s)?

6. What are the things I learned about relationships from my religion and/or culture(s) that *haven't* helped me in my adult life?

7. What are the things I learned about relationships from my religion and/or culture(s) that *have* helped me in my adult life?

Jean's Answers

1. What did I learn from my religion and/or culture(s) I grew up in about intimate relationships?

I grew up in the Catholic faith in a small rural Canadian town. In the church, I was taught that it was a sin to lose your virginity before you were married and that you were supposed to wait until marriage to have sex. I was also taught that divorce is a sin and that once you marry, it's for life.

2. What was my expected role in relationships as a woman?

I was taught to be like the Virgin Mary; quiet, demure, submissive, and angelic. I was taught to put everyone else's needs before my own and that my happiness would come from taking care of others and being selfless.

3. What was I taught by my religion and/or culture(s) to expect and not expect in relationships?

I was taught that I could depend on a man to take care of me financially when I married him. Also, that he would protect me from harm. I wasn't taught to expect him to treat me as an equal and that we would be best friends before spouses.

4. What was I taught by my religion and/or culture(s) about what would happen to me if I didn't abide by their rules/beliefs/values about relationships?

I was taught that a woman must stay married and have children in order to be 'respectable' and that if she left her husband, she was a "sinner" and would be punished by God. If I chose not to have children and wanted to have a career and work outside the home, I would be considered "unfeminine" and somehow suspect. They wouldn't see me as a good role model for younger Catholic girls.

5. How have my choices of partners as an adult been influenced by what I learned from my religion and/or culture(s)?

I chose a man who I thought was a "good Catholic" who would take care of me financially and protect me from harm. I believed that once we were married, we would be together until the end.

6. What are the things I learned about relationships from my religion and/or culture(s) that *haven't* helped me in my adult life?

- *That divorce is a sin and that you should stay in a marriage even when it's not good for you or your children*

- *Rigid sex-roles for men and woman — following them made me and my husband miserable and ended up ruining the relationship*

7. What are the things I learned about relationships from my religion and/or culture(s) that *have* helped me in my adult life?

- *That you shouldn't give up on people easily and that relationships are sacred*

- *That relationships work better when you share a spiritual path with your partner*

Step Four: Change Your "Self-Talk"

I'm going to share a very simple but highly effective concept with you. Are you ready to learn what thousands of therapists, coaches, and personal trainers use as the basis of making a hefty living off of others? Here it is....

WHAT YOU TELL YOURSELF ABOUT WHAT YOU DESERVE AND CAN ACHIEVE IS EXACTLY WHAT YOU GET.

I bet you're thinking, "That isn't rocket science!" That's very true – it isn't. However, I'm guessing that if you bought this book; you're not utilizing this concept to it's full potential in the area of relationships and could use a refresher course. Let me give you an example of what I'm talking about. I was working with a young woman dating a guy who treated her like dirt. He was verbally and physically abusive towards her and she felt really miserable when she was with him.

When I asked her if she felt she deserved to be treated this way, she answered "no." But when I asked her why she didn't try dating a nice guy who treated her with respect and dignity, she just looked at me blankly and said, "There are guys like that?" Not only did she not notice the nice guys, but also when pressed further, she told me she didn't believe that someone like that would be attracted to her. In her mind, she was telling herself that she deserved the losers for boyfriends and that being with jerks was the only possibility available to her. In this example, **what she told herself about what she deserved and could achieve is exactly what she got**.

Let me ask you a question:

Do you truly believe that (a) it is possible to have a fabulous relationship with the partner of your dreams; and, (b) that you deserve to have that?

Be really honest with yourself here. My experience tells me that most of us are not able to answer a resounding "yes" to both of these questions when first asked. There are many reasons for that; many of which I outlined earlier in the first section of this book. The great thing is that we don't need to understand WHY we have erroneous beliefs in order to change them for the better. All we have to do is change what we say to ourselves. So let's get started...

Self-Talk Relationship Worksheet

In this next exercise, I'm going to encourage you to take a good look at what you are currently telling yourself about relationships, have an argument with yourself, and then come up with more positive self-talk about relationships. This process will show you how silly or flawed your self-talk is, give you some alternatives, as well as a chance to change your self-talk into positive affirmations which will prepare your psyche and entire being for a wonderful and fulfilling relationship with a great partner someday. **Do not underestimate the power of your thoughts.** Remember:

WHAT YOU TELL YOURSELF ABOUT WHAT YOU DESERVE AND CAN ACHIEVE IS EXACTLY WHAT YOU GET.

In order to fill this in, it may be helpful to start each sentence with something like, "I believe…" or "I deserve…" or "It's not possible…" in the first column to get in touch with your core beliefs about what you believe about relationships. In the second column, you get to have a good argument with yourself (very therapeutic!) and will write down all the counter-arguments to the points in the first column. Then in the third column, you'll turn negative self-talk about relationships into positives. The third column is the 'gold', as these will become your mantras that will allow you to attract your ideal partner in the future. It works! How do I know? Because this is exactly the process I used, as well as many of my clients, to attract an ideal partner. See Jean's example if you're stuck.

What I tell myself now about relationships	Why that's not true	What I will tell myself from now on about relationships

What I tell myself now about relationships	Why that's not true	What I will tell myself from now on about relationships

Sample: Jean's Worksheet

What I tell myself *now* about relationships	Why that's not true	What I will tell myself *from now on* about relationships
I believe that all men are jerks and treat women badly.	I know a few really good men who treat their girlfriends/ wives really well like: Michael, Robert, and Julio.	There are lots of men out there who are really good people and treat women with dignity, respect, and caring.
I don't deserve a loving, fulfilling relationship because I'm so flawed.	Just because I have a few "quirks" and am working through issues in my life doesn't exclude me from	I'm not perfect, but I'm good enough. I'm human and as such, deserve all the best that life has to offer, including a loving, ful- filling relationship.

	being deserving of a great relationship. We're all flawed. That's what makes us human.	
	And, we also deserve great relationships.	
It's not possible for me to have a loving, fulfilling long-term relationship – it only happens in the movies.	*Just because I haven't had one of these types of relationships doesn't mean they aren't possible. Gina at work has a loving, fulfilling long-term relation-*	*It is entirely possible for me to have a loving, fulfilling long-term relationship. In fact, it's on its way right now!*

	ship with her husband and she's not a movie star.	
It's impossible for me to have a great relationship because I came from a dysfunctional family and have no role models of that type of relationship.	*Just because I didn't grow up seeing these types of relationships all around me doesn't mean I can't find role models for them now as an adult. I know lots of couples that have the kind of relationship I want that can serve as role models.*	*It's never too late to learn from positive, healthy role models. I am attracting a multitude of inspirational role models for healthy relationships which will guide me on my way to creating a similar relationship.*

It's safer to just stay single. That way, I'm guaranteed not to get hurt anymore in relationships.	*That may be true, but I don't want to be single for the rest of my life. Yes, it's true that I could get hurt again, but that's all part of the package of finding the right mate. It's a risk that's worth taking.*	*Getting hurt is part of living. I'm willing to risk feeling uncomfortable in order to attract my ideal life partner someday.*

I recommend that you buy a stack of index cards and write each affirmation from the third column on one index card. When you've created a little pile of relationship affirmations, be sure to read them out loud once in the morning upon awakening and then once before sleep each night. Brain research shows that these are the times of day when the brain is the most suggestible and able to take in new information. If you still have a "chump" sleeping next to you, you may want to read your affirmations silently or in another room (just a hint to make your life easier!)

Step Five: Figure Out Who You Are and What Your Needs Are

After you've started re-working your self-talk about what's possible for you in relationships and are using your daily affirmations to attract the ideal partner, you can work on a few other areas that will ensure your success. I realize this may sound basic, but one of the best methods I've come across to attract an ideal mate is to look for someone **a lot like you**. Do I need a Masters degree to know that? Probably not. However, my personal and professional experience assisting countless women to find an ideal partner with great successes tells me that it works!

To give you an example, I am working with a young woman right now who is dissatisfied with the guys she dates. When we examined it closely, it turns out that she picks a particular type of guy every time who is generally: uninterested in her, a partier, non-committal, and doesn't care to really get to know who she is and what makes her happy. Sound familiar? Yep – there's a lot of them out there.

This beautiful young woman is extremely intelligent, sensitive, caring, and committed to relationships in her life. When I asked her if the losers she keeps picking are anything like her, she looked at me oddly and said, "Uh... no..." I then proceeded to ask her what she thought it would be like if she were to date someone who had a similar personality to hers and similar interests. She looked dumbfounded and said, "Well that would be great but I never thought about picking someone like me."

So there you have it, gals. I think most of us are like this young woman. We have such a narrow definition of the "type" of person we date, that we often have trouble thinking 'outside the box' to explore other, more satisfying, possibilities.

And I'm not just speaking as a therapist here – I used this exact formula for attracting the ideal partner and it worked wonders! I had always dated guys who were totally incompatible with me, but had never given it a second thought until I stopped dating for a while and examined with a flashlight my patterns in relationships and what was getting me into trouble every time. Compatibility is not to be underestimated! I read somewhere that 95% of life happiness is based on choosing the right partner and while that's a pretty extreme statistic, I think the general point is valid. Just think about how much of your time and energy is sucked up when you're with the wrong person? Need I say more?

One more point while we're on this topic of choosing an ideal mate: how many times have you actually **chosen** the person you ended up with? My experience tells me that most of us do not actively choose the people we end up in relationships with. They usually *find us* and we think something like, "Oh, wow. Someone is interested in me. I'm so flattered. I guess I'll give them a chance." It isn't very often that we take a good hard look at who this person is and who we are, and then make a sound judgment call about whether a relationship with them would be a good thing or not.

I think we're far too quick to leap into relationships with both feet without thinking things through from the beginning. You've probably got to admit that when you take a really honest look at the relationships you've had that didn't work out, you had a gut feeling right at the beginning that it wasn't a good match, but you didn't listen to yourself. If you get one thing out of reading this book and doing the exercises contained within, I hope it's that you **learn to trust your gut feelings about someone when you first meet them and can listen to what they are telling you**. It will end up saving you a lot of time and aggravation in the long run.

I will list some 'red flags' that appeared from the get-go from some of my client's stories, that popped up everywhere telling them the person wasn't a good match but they chose to ignore them anyway:

"He walked ahead of me when we were going somewhere."

"She didn't even pretend to be interested in what I had to say."

"He told me that he wasn't physically attracted to me."

"She always talked about herself and never listened to me."

"He got really mad at me for something insignificant on our second date."

My advice? **Watch, notice, and listen to the red flags right from the start!** It will help you to 'weed out' the losers a lot faster so that you can devote your precious time to finding the winners!

Here are some questions you can answer which will help you to figure out who might be the right kind of match for you as a partner. I've included Jean's example answers again to assist you if you're stuck.

Exercise: Figuring Out Who You Are and What Your Needs Are in a Mate

1. What is my personality type?

2. What are my hobbies and interests?

3. What kinds of people bring out the best in me?

4. What kinds of people have I been dating and do they bring out the best in me and fit with who I am?

Jean's Answers

1. What is my personality type?

I'm quiet, sensitive to things around me, and I like to be alone quite a bit. I enjoy people, but also need time away from others in order to 'recharge my batteries.'

2. What are my hobbies and interests?

Reading, doing yoga, watching old films, listening to soul-stirring music, walking in nature, and cooking.

3. What kinds of people bring out the best in me?

People who love and appreciate me for who I am and who like doing similar things. I like to be around people who are comfortable being silent together at times, and who also enjoy lively conversation when they're in the mood.

4. What kind of people have I been dating and do they bring out the best in me and fit with who I am?

The complete opposite of who I am! I've dated loud, non-stop talkers who like to party and go out all the time and think I'm weird for wanting to be quiet and do things at home or without others. These guys make me feel like I'm a freak because of who I am and are constantly criticizing me and saying I should be more like them. This leaves me feeling really crappy about myself, misunderstood, and not appreciated. It also lowers my self-esteem big-time. Because we're so different, we're constantly fighting and not having a good time. I don't like who I become when I'm with them because I'm not nice and I get all nit-picky and negative. They definitely don't bring out the best in me and are not a fit with my personality.

Step Six: Start Becoming the Kind of Person You Want to Attract

I don't want to insult your intelligence here, but this step is not as simple as it may sound on the surface. In the step right after this one, I'm going to give you a chance to really figure out what kind of person you eventually want to attract. But before we go there, I feel that it is absolutely imperative that you first figure out **how you're going to attract the fabulous partner you want and deserve.** "How do I do that?" you may be asking.

The only answer I have that makes any sense to me and has worked over and over again for so many women I've worked with is this: **start becoming the kind of person you want to attract.** If you really think about it, it makes a lot of sense. I mean, how are you going to attract someone fabulous if you don't already believe that YOU are fabulous and deserving of someone wonderful?

If you're walking around with your head hung down saying, "I'm not so great, really. I've got so many faults…" and blah, blah,

blah… do you think some fabulous potential partner is going to come running to you screaming, "I absolutely have to have you! By what you're saying, I'm convinced that I want to have an intimate relationship with you!"

Not bloody likely, say I.

It may be helpful here to use an example. I had a client, who was in the post-menopausal stage of her life, who said that her main goal in therapy was "to have a healthy relationship." She had already been through multiple marriages to severely abusive alcoholics, from whom she had narrowly escaped. When we looked at her family-of-origin, she had grown up in a highly dysfunctional family where she had never learned about healthy relationships and basically learned that relationships are about tolerating abuse in exchange for financial security.

When I asked her questions about what she was looking for in a mate and what she considered "healthy" to be, she drew a complete blank (how many of us can identify with this?). I explained that a key step for her was to become "healthy" herself in order to attract another "healthy" person as a partner.

For this particular woman, she defined a healthy relationship as being one in which no one was playing games with the other or bartering for things they wanted that the other person had. It was really important for her to feel equal to her partner, and to know that the reason they were together would simply be because they enjoyed being together; not because they were trying to "get" something from the other.

Also, it was really important to her that the next partner she chose would NOT be abusive and/or an alcoholic or addicted to anything else. She was absolutely fed up with dealing with abuse and alcoholism and all of the problems that came along with these issues.

So when I asked her how she was going to become her 'half' of the deal in what she wanted in a future relationship, more blanks. So that's where we started the work – just looking at *her* and how *she* could become the kind of woman that would attract her ideal mate.

One area that she worked really hard on was letting go of her concept of what a "relationship" between a man and woman looked like. She had never experienced a relationship wherein there wasn't some sort of barter going on.

She did a lot of hard work in therapy, exploring her version of reality when it came to relationships, and was eventually able to imagine a different kind of relationship for herself that felt a whole lot better than the ones she had experienced in the past. She began to see that women and men could coexist without playing games with each other or 'using' the other person or letting themselves be 'used'.

One of her first steps was to stop using men in relationships to get financial security. This was an enormous step for her because she had never had the experience of supporting herself financially without the help of a man. She was terrified of taking the leap of becoming financially independent, but went ahead anyway and is well on her way to meeting that goal.

Once she started to make her own money and support herself, she soon realized that she didn't need a man to make ends meet financially and this really threw her for a psychological loop. She then began to ask herself what the point would be of having a man in her life if she didn't need his money. The answers really surprised her, but in a very good way. She realized that what she really wanted in a relationship was companionship; to have someone to share the ups and downs of life with.

This realization brought up a lot of sadness as she got in touch with the fact that she'd never experienced that in an intimate relationship before and that is what she had wanted all along, but hadn't been conscious of. At the same time, it gave her a lot of hope because she had discovered something vital that would help in her search for a healthy partnership in the future.

She started to look at men as potential "companions" rather than "financial providers" and guess what? She was looking at men she never would have considered in the past! This turned out to be a great thing!

Exercise: Becoming the Kind of Partner I Want to Attract

For this exercise, I'm going to invite your "inner child" out for an evening of fun, learning, and exploration. This exercise involves a "role play" of sorts and to do it effectively, you'll have to gather your friends around. In terms of what I'm going to ask you to do, I think that the slogan from 12-step traditions; "fake it until you make it" applies.

What I'm inviting you to do here is exactly that. PRETEND to be the fabulous new you bursting with self-esteem, confidence, and inner calm, who would be a total "magnet" to a fabulous potential mate. In my life, I have learned on many occasions a basic mathematical equation:

$$SUCCESS = CONFIDENCE$$

In other words, BE the person you know you really are inside and ACT as if you deserve only the very best. Guess what? Your brain doesn't know the difference! Even if you don't believe that you are kind, loving, and beautiful, you can pretend that you do and the rest will follow suit!

So here's a chance to play "dress-up" and "pretend" as an adult!

Instructions:

Invite some like-minded friends over who are also trying to attract better partners. Make sure it's an even number so people can pair off into two's. When you call to invite them, say that you're working on letting go of dating the wrong people and that you want to share a special exercise with them to help them do the same. Make sure you tell them it will be a fun evening and to dress up!

Prepare 'the scene' as a 'date' atmosphere – perhaps make your living room into a small café or park. Set up areas for pairings of two and make sure you place the seats facing each other. Also, make sure you get a timer that makes a sound when the time is up – you'll need one that can go for at least 15 minutes.

When your guests arrive, welcome them and supply each person with a few sheets of blank paper and a pen. Tell them that they have half an hour to prepare a 15-minute written monologue about **why they are a fabulous catch and what they have to offer another person in a long-term relationship.**

Give the following instructions: Go wild and really embellish here! Write things that make you feel like you're totally bragging about yourself and which make you even squirm a bit – that's how you'll know you're on target. Write down as many fabulous things about yourself as possible until you have none left. Pretend you're a PR specialist and what you're promoting is YOU!

Be prepared to meet your own internal resistance. This is possibly one of the hardest things we can ever ask of ourselves. It's extremely easy to say nice things about *other* people and to rave on and on about *their* great qualities, but quite another to do the same for ourselves. That's okay. This isn't *supposed* to be easy – it's meant to help you grow into the fabulous person you really are –

the one who's been waiting backstage all these years. It's time to let her out and give her center stage!

Pair people off and have them sit in different corners of the room at their individual "spaces" that you've set up before-hand and give them the following instructions:

*I'm going to set the timer for 15 minutes and one person in your pair has to share their "Why I'm a Great Catch/What I have to Offer a Fabulous Partner" speech. You must keep talking for the **entire** 15 minutes. This means that if you run out of items on your list, you'll need to add new ones. Your partner can acknowledge you by saying very brief things like, "Wow" or "That's incredible" but that is to be the extent of their feedback. The point of the exercise is to allow you to really talk about yourself and say great things about who you are and what you have to offer in a relationship. When the timer makes its sound, we'll switch partners and do the same.*

Once everyone has had a chance to complete the exercise, gather everyone into a circle and end by asking each person to state one positive thing that they gained by doing the exercise.

Have a little party and have some fun!

Step Seven: Create a Strong Image of Your Ideal Partner

Remember the cardinal rule from earlier on in this book:

WHAT YOU TELL YOURSELF ABOUT WHAT

YOU DESERVE AND CAN ACHIEVE IS

EXACTLY WHAT YOU GET.

This principle is of utmost importance when it comes to visualizing your ideal partner and making 'a space' in your psyche for them. This concept is tied into the whole 'affirmation' thing and it works! One of my favourite stories that I tell people about meeting my husband is about "Esther's Man Checklist."

It goes something like this: I was fed up with dating the wrong guys and wasting time in unfulfilling, stress-inducing relationships. During my five years of being 'consciously single' and preparing myself for a healthy long-term partnership, I came up with a "Man Checklist" that I could use when I started dating again to see if people were worth pursuing or not. I think I had 15 items in total.

To this day, I am amazed that when I met my husband, I checked off every single one of them! No kidding. This is actually fact.

I think this example speaks volumes about the power of doing the preparation work I'm sharing with you in this book in order to receive the kind of partner and relationship you really want. And when he showed up, I actually wasn't surprised because I had worked so hard at attracting someone like him. It just seemed to make perfect sense that he arrived and that we began the most loving, fulfilling, and fun relationship that either of us had ever had.

Does that story motivate you or make you want to retch? Either reaction is fine. But if you want to retch, you may need to do a little more work on believing that a wonderful relationship is possible for you and will manifest if you so choose.

So to help you along, I'm going to share my "famous checklist" method with you. I hope it works as well for you as it has for me and so many other women I know. Even if you're skeptical, give it a try. It will only take about half an hour of your time and it's fun to fantasize! I've given you an example from Jean again if you get stuck.

It's pretty straightforward. In the "Characteristics" column, write what it is you're looking for in a partner – if you have more than 15, photocopy the blank list and fill it in. Then put a star in either the "Negotiable" or "Non-negotiable" column to remind you how important each characteristic is. After you've completed the list, try it out on people you date. For each characteristic that they meet, put a checkmark in the first column.

My Ideal Partner Checklist

√	Characteristics	Negotiable	Non-negotiable

√	Characteristics	Negotiable	Non-negotiable

Jean's Ideal Partner Checklist

√	Characteristics	Negotiable	Non-negotiable
	Sensitive		*
	Kind		*
	Good sense of humour		*
	Likes cooking	*	
	Enjoys the same kind of music as me	*	
	Communicates his feelings		*
	Loves to dance		*

√	Characteristics	Negotiable	Non-negotiable
	Has a career and earns a decent amount of money		*
	Has done family-of-origin work and continues to do so		*
	Sexy and good-looking		*
	Reliable		*
	Wants a long-term relationship		*
	Loves animals	*	

√	Characteristics	Negotiable	Non-negotiable
	Intellectual		*
	Has women friends who think he's a great person		*

Step Eight: Study People Who Meet the Criteria of Your Ideal Partner

This next step is pretty straightforward. I'll start by asking you a question: How does someone become a great musician? If you're answer is "practice, practice, practice" you've got part of it. Yes, one must practice over and over again until they get the result they are looking for. But equally important is this:

THEY STUDY THE GREAT MUSICIANS

AND LEARN FROM THEM.

How does this apply to finding your ideal partner? It's really very basic. If you've grown up with unhealthy relationship role models (your parents, for example) and then followed their lead and had one miserable relationship after another, you probably need new role models.

Here's an example to illustrate my point: A client of mine (let's call her Beth), had recently left an abusive relationship that she had been in for 16 years. She was extremely wary of men and had a hard time believing there were any decent ones out there for her to choose from in the future.

When we explored her family-of-origin experiences, it was evident that she had no role models for healthy relationships between men and women when she was growing up. Her father had been abusive to her mother and her mother never left him. Ditto with her grandparents as well as aunts and uncles. She realized that she had learned from her family that in intimate relationships between men and women, there was no equality, sharing of responsibilities, or respect for one another.

At one point Beth looked at my wide-eyed and asked, "If that's all I know, how am I ever going to have a different kind of relationship?"

My answer: "Study people who have what you want in relationships. Pretend you're in school – take notes, ask lots of questions, listen, observe, and learn."

So off she went to study the kind of relationship she herself wanted some day. The results were astounding! In a very short time, she came to realize that there were a number of really good men out there who treated women really well and as equals. The more she searched them out, the more couples she found who were enjoying loving, healthy, and fulfilling relationships.

She befriended many of these couples and studied them intensely. She asked them questions about how they met, what they felt they deserved in relationships, and about their keys to success in relationships. She got so much wonderful feedback and made many new friends. Not only that, but they constantly validated her desire to have a healthy relationship someday and helped her believe that it was entirely possible. Her healing and growth were tremendous.

To begin this process, it will be helpful for you to write a list of all of the healthy couples you know who have the kind of relationship you want. (A blank list can be found on the following pages). Think way back – even to childhood – bring to consciousness all of the positive, loving, and healthy relationships you can remember witnessing. Don't panic if none of these are family members: that is often the case.

If so, look outside of your family to other people in your extended community. If you don't find any of these 'relationship role models' there either, do not be discouraged. They are sometimes hard to find. You may have to sleuth them out just like a good detective would. You may have to find your role models in books, films, or even on television. Just make sure that they are realistic!

Healthy Relationships List

| |
| |
| |
| |
| |
| |
| |
| |

Step Nine: Become Friends With People Who Meet Your Criteria

Another very important step in the process of finding your ideal mate is to **learn to be friends** with someone suitable for partnership before you jump into a romantic relationship with them. This may seem like an odd idea to you, as it does to many of the women I know. However, I urge you to give it a solid try before dismissing it altogether.

The concept of being friends with someone who has partner potential came to me in my late 20s when I was searching for my ideal mate. I realized one day with great clarity that most of the guys I had dated in the past *weren't even suitable for friendship*. I then thought, "If I didn't even want to be *friends* with this person, what made me think that I'd want to have an even closer relationship with them?"

If you think about it, it makes a lot of sense. When you pick your friends, do you overlook many characteristics that you don't like in them and pick people who you have nothing in common with?

If your answer is "yes", than you need to work on your friendships as well as your intimate relationships! If your answer is a resounding "no", then you probably get what I'm talking about here.

I once heard a tape of Marianne Williamson, who is a teacher of *"A Course In Miracles"* (a course of study I highly recommend), speaking about women and intimate relationships. She used an analogy that I really like. She said that an intimate relationship is like a long-stemmed rose: the stem represents the friendship and the rose blossom represents the romantic aspect of the relationship. She says that without a solid stem, the rose cannot blossom.

In other words, without a solid base of friendship, the chances of having a healthy, fulfilling, and long-term romantic relationship are quite low. I realize that it doesn't always work this way, say in the case of an arranged marriage. But even in such instances, after the couple is married and gets to know one another really well and become good friends, the romantic aspect often blossoms more and becomes more fulfilling over time.

When I do my own research and ask happy couples who have been together for a long time what the key to their success is, I constantly get the same answer back: **"We are best friends."** Note they don't say, "The sex is awesome." Or, "It's always so exciting." While that may well be the case, I would argue that those things are possible **because they have a solid base of friendship** underlying everything else and that the friendship is of supreme importance.

Just before I met my husband over seven years ago, I had made a very firm decision that I was going to be friends with a man for at least three months before I got romantically involved. I figured that this would prevent me from leaping into a not-so-great relationship with full force before I had time to really assess whether this person would be an ideal partner or not.

In the past, I had done just the opposite, like so many of us do. I would feel the initial attraction (or their attraction to me), and would basically just jump into a romantic relationship. When I look back on all of those relationships now, I realize that I probably would have given **at least half of them a miss** if I had given myself the *luxury of time* to assess whether we were a good match for each other. I sure could have saved myself a lot of stress, heartbreak, and aggravation!

I can hear the counter-argument already: "But then you wouldn't have learned so much and you are the person you are today because of all the mistakes you made." Well, yeah – that is true, but don't you think there comes a point in each woman's life when she has *learned enough*? I mean, how many darn 'growth experiences' do we actually need in order to learn our lesson?

I decided that I'd learned enough of what didn't work – thank you very much– and it was time to be happy and to enjoy a really great relationship for once. I'm sure glad I did because if I had played it differently, I could be sitting here in my mid-30s in yet another soul-sucking relationship that would leave me very little time or energy to do what I love in life.

Perhaps the whole 'becoming friends first' concept is alien to you. Most likely, it is because you were taught such a warped concept of 'romantic love'. It usually goes something like this: Girl meets boy. They feel all mushy inside, while at the same time wanting desperately to 'jump each others bones'. They can't keep away from each other or focus on anything else in their lives and essentially morph into this codependent, narcissistic blob which they (and everyone else around them) calls "love." There is no "I" and "you," but just "we."

Hallmark makes a fortune selling this collective delusion we mistakenly call "love." It's the stuff that all of those bubble-gum pop songs are based on. My personal favourite is the one that goes, "*I can't live, if living is without you...*" I don't know about you, but if a guy said that to me now, I'd be giving him a therapist's business card and changing my phone number so fast he wouldn't know what had happened!

I also want to let you in on another bit of wisdom while we're on the subject:

IF A PERSON ISN'T ABLE OR WILLING TO BE YOUR FRIEND FOR A WHILE BEFORE JUMPING INTO BED WITH YOU, THEY MOST LIKELY ARE NOT YOUR IDEAL PARTNER.

People who express a great urgency to jump into a romantic relationship have "red flag" written all over their forehead (just a little visual you may want to use). A question to ask yourself about them is, "What's the big rush?" Often, it's a sign that someone isn't comfortable being in their own skin, doesn't know themselves or like themselves that much, and is looking for someone else to make them happy. If you sense this is the case, do yourself a big favour, and HEAD FOR THE HILLS!

If it's a healthy, whole person you want to partner up with, there should be no urgency there. People who are solid within themselves are happy whether they are single or in a relationship because:

THEY ENJOY THEIR OWN COMPANY AND HAVE A FULL LIFE REGARDLESS OF WHETHER THEY HAVE A PARTNER OR NOT.

Don't think you're exempt from meeting the same requirements yourself. If you're looking for someone else to complete you because you're not solid and happy within yourself, you're not going to attract someone healthy. A healthy person would meet you and head for the hills!

If you think about it, it makes a lot of sense:

WE ATTRACT OTHERS WHO ARE AT THE SAME EMOTIONAL LEVEL THAT WE ARE AT.

I paid a hell of a lot of money in therapy training to learn that, so you're getting a great deal here!

If we're needy, codependent, and unhappy with ourselves, we'll attract someone just like us. On the other hand, if we are happy and whole in ourselves and are looking for someone to enhance **the already rich and full life we have,** we'll attract someone just like us.

Step Ten: Date Until You Find Your Ideal Partner

At last! You've forged your way uphill through the first nine steps and are finally reaching the top of the mountain! But, alas, before you get there and can bask in the glory of the beautiful view, you've got one more piece of work to do…

In this last step, you get to put all of your hard work to good use and take you're show on the road! I see this phase as practicing being a good "researcher" in the dating department. This is the time to take a step back from the way you used to date and instead, become a little bit 'cooler', and much more thoughtful. I also encourage you to SLOW DOWN – imagining that you're dating in slow-motion; everything moves at much more of a 'Zen' pace – slowly, thoughtfully, and mindfully.

This should feel extremely weird and uncomfortable at first. You may not even recognize yourself at times! That's a good sign! You're adopting a **whole new way** of doing the dating thing and it's going to take some getting used to. But do not despair; the angst is worth it! You may not find your ideal partner as quickly as you would like, and you may have to date a number of different people before getting to them, but like that old adage says, "The best things in life are worth waiting for."

As someone who has gone through this same process and who now enjoys a wonderful, fulfilling relationship every day, let me tell you that this is very true indeed. When I was consciously single for five years in order to become the kind of person that I wanted to attract, I decided that I'd rather be lonely than in a miserable, unfulfilling relationship. I'm guessing you're at that point too…

Here are some key points to follow when you start the dating process and are on the road to meeting the fabulous partner you want and deserve:

1. There's no rush!

This is not an emergency! No one has ever died from being single! You're not settling for what just happens to come along anymore, so your criteria for suitable mates have shrunk. Go for *quality, not quantity* when it comes to dates.

Refer back to your exercises from this book often as you date and ask yourself whether there are any "red flags" jumping out at you. Especially refer to your "checklist" when you're considering someone (best to do this before even agreeing to a date so that you won't waste time on people who don't have the major characteristics you're looking for). Remember that you're severely narrowing down the number of people you would choose to even go on a date with because now you have a clearer idea of the kind of person you're looking for.

2. Be kind and gentle with yourself the whole way through.

This is so important as you begin dating because you'll feel vulnerable and may need extra doses of self-care when things don't work out or you make a mistake along the way. And remember – mistakes are allowed! In fact, expect them and you'll be better able to deal with them. Dating is difficult and can bring with it a lot of emotional ups and downs. Pace yourself and be kind to yourself by not expecting perfection. Sometimes it helps to remember that the person you're dating is also going through a similar process.

3. Learn to be "old fashioned."

Without sounding all Victorian, what I mean by that is GO SLOWLY as you date. Become friends with the person before getting intimately involved. Whatever you do, DO NOT JUMP INTO BED WITH SOMEONE when you're just getting to know them. Sex totally complicates things and takes things to an entirely different level. Remember what I said earlier: a good prospective partner will have no problem being friends before getting sexual. In fact, that's a very good sign that they are potential partner material. If they're not instantly groping at your body and are more interested in casually getting to know you as a person, they are telling you that it's not just sex they're after and that you're more than just a body to them. Many of the women I've counselled tell me that one of the biggest differences between their new healthy partners and the old unhealthy ones was the fact that they didn't leap into bed together before really getting to know one another first.

4. Check in regularly with those who know you and love you the most.

I honestly don't know what I'd do without my incredible friends as well as some very wise family members! Sometimes when you're dating, you can temporarily lose perspective and essentially, forget who you are and what you're looking for in a mate. So make sure you set up a "dating support team" to help you stay on track. In fact, I urge you to give copies of your "ideal partner checklist" to the people who you trust the most and who really want to see you in a healthy, fulfilling relationship someday. When you call them to debrief a date, ask them to refer to their copy of your checklist to give you feedback and to remind you of what you're looking for in a mate.

5. *Use your sense of humour!*

Trust me – you'll need it! Mate selection can be a whole lot easier and more enjoyable if you don't take the whole thing too seriously. Don't get me wrong – you must be serious about finding the right partner – but approaching the whole dating aspect with some humour and a sense of fun can make things a whole let better.

6. *Keep dates short and sweet at the beginning.*

One way to make dating easier and lighter is to plan short dates for the first couple of dates. I say no more than two hours for a first date. In fact, it's usually a good idea to have other plans immediately following your date. That way, you have an "out" if you know fairly quickly that this person isn't potential partner material. It also shows you're not desperate and that you have a life! I don't know about you, but for me, a big turn-off is someone who appears needy and doesn't have much else going on in their life besides looking for a mate. A DEFINITE RED FLAG!

7. Don't tell them that you've done this workbook and especially, don't share your checklist with them!

I'm guessing that you wouldn't even think of doing this, but you never can be too careful. And furthermore, this kind of talk is entirely inappropriate for a first date. You want to keep things light at first and simply *experience* how you feel when you're around this person. Get a good sense of them and how you interact with each other. Have some fun and enjoy the experience.

CLOSING

So there you have it, my dear sisters. I've wracked my brain, delved into my own heart and the experiences of women I've worked with over the years, and given you what I hope will be very useful information, as well as tools that will assist you on your journey to finding your ideal partner.

At the very least, I hope that I've made you laugh and given you some food for thought. I'd love to hear feedback from you about this book and how it did or didn't work for you. I, too, am learning as I go and really appreciate constructive feedback on how I can improve books for future editions.

I'd also love to hear your experiences with following these steps! Send me your story when you've "dumped that chump" and/or met your ideal partner, to be shared with others on my website. Please also attach photos if you feel like it as I'd love to create a "happy couples" page on the book's website. When you send in your story, you will automatically be entered into a draw to win an e-book I wrote called, *What Your Mama Can't or Won't Teach You: Grown Women's Stories of Their Teen Years.* You can email your story to me at esther@estherkane.com. I look forward to hearing about your success!

Printed in the United States
61602LVS00002B/52-150